Why I Stu... My Arse ...

For Mum and Dad

Character List

Billy
Adam
Wine Gum
Dad
Daisy
Elton John
Mr Kripson
Mrs Richards
Finnian
Rodney
Chris Tingle
Mrs Beaver
Ben Shephard, *as himself*
Chris Kamara, *as himself*
Simon Jules, *alternate radio host*

Notes on the Text

Why I Stuck a Flare Up My Arse for England is inspired by real events that took place on the day of the UEFA European Championship Final between England and Italy on Sunday 11 July 2021. All characters depicted in the play are entirely fictionalised.

The story is told through Billy's perspective. He serves as narrator and, at times, steps into the roles of other characters around him. The only voices not performed live by Billy are the **radio hosts, the commentators** and **Adam's voicemail**.

For the 2025 Edinburgh Fringe production, **Ben Shephard** and **Chris Kamara** lent their voices to the radio hosts, and the main script has been updated to reflect their inclusion. The **original radio scene** with a fictional host is retained at the end of the text as an alternate.

Throughout the play, Billy occasionally breaks into football chants. These moments act as transitions or emotional outbursts, punctuating key shifts in the narrative.

Prologue

Sunday 11 July 2021

Wembley Way.

An FA Pyro Facts Poster that says: 'Que Sera, Sera, whatever will be, will be, you're going to A&E.'

Billy *enters. Head to toe in England gear, can of Stella in hand, bucket hat and all. He rips the poster down.*

This is anti-fun propaganda!

He crushes the can on his head and dances hard to 'Vindaloo' by Fat Les.

Diehards.

The lot of us.

All packed into this glorious stretch of land they call *Wembley Way.*

Proud to be here.

Proud to be one.

Proud to be *English.*

Three lions on our shirt.

Hoping and praying that this will be the night that ends all the hurt.

No rules today . . .

No one saying that you can't do anything . . .

be anything.

Bottles are being flung across the sky

People are swinging out from lampposts up high

We're throwing fences!

Flipping benches!

Police are getting jittery.

WE ARE GONNA DO ITALY!

Billy *turns his attention to the red smoke flare in front of him.*

My turn to do something crazy.

My turn to be seen.

To walk upon England's mountains green.

Announcing to the crowd, flare high up above his head.

THIS FLARE IS GOING UP MY BUM. AND WHY? WHY
. . .

BECAUSE IT'S FUCKING FUN!

All the boys are egging me on

Cheering, laughing, and singing their songs

My mate Wine Gum leading the pack

Beaming like a Christmas tree as I perform my act.

I pull my pants down as the crowd starts to cheer,

Wine Gum cracks open his twenty-fourth beer!

I catch a glimpse of the hundreds of people looking at me.

And in that moment, I know what it is to just *be*.

So I give the people what they wanna see

Filling their faces with delightful glee

And as I pass the flare from hand to crack

Like a relay race on an Olympic track

A final bump of coke, to speak a statement everyone will
admire

FOR ENGLAND.

FOR ST GEORGE.

AND FOR

HARRY MAGUIRE!

And in a swift, valiant, gladiatorial way . . .

Billy Kinley *sticks the flare up his arse.*

Blackout as we hear distant crowds chanting 'BILLY'S ON FIRE, AND HIS RECTUM'S TERRIFIED!' to the tune of 'Freed from Desire' by Gala.

–

Lights up on **Billy** *in his bedroom. The morning after the night before.* **Billy** *can barely keep his eyes open; he is deeply hungover.*

Ben Shephard   Welcome back to Fanatic about Footie with me, Ben Shephard!

Chris Kamara   And me, Chris Kamara.

Ben Shephard   Well, despair sweeps the nation this morning as last night's Euros final against Italy ended in bitter disappointment. Kammy, tough one to take, wasn't it?

Chris Kamara   Absolutely, I am gutted, Ben. Really gutted. I had so much hope in the build-up.

Ben Shephard   Well, someone else who had a lot of hope was Mr Billy Kinley, who was pictured, before the game on Wembley Way, doing something pretty explosive!

They both laugh for just long enough before it becomes a bit too much.

Ben Shephard   And he's joined us on the phone now! Billy – care to explain to the listener what you did?

Billy   Yeah, I stuck a flare up my bum.

Chris Kamara   Unbelievable.

Ben Shephard   It really is, unbelievable.

Chris Kamara   Billy you've got over 50,000 likes on Instagram and hashtag bum flare man is still trending on Twitter!

Billy   That's right, Kammy. I guess I'm a bit of a cult hero.

Ben Shephard   Can I just ask you, Billy, what does it feel like when you're sticking a flare up your arse?

Billy   I can't really explain it . . .

Beat.

Chris Kamara   It looks like he hasn't got the words . . .

Billy *quotes a key line from the movie 'Billy Elliot' about losing who you are.*

Ben Shephard   Is that Billy Elliot?

Billy   No! My name's Kinley. It's Billy Kin – Ley!

Chris Kamara   So, why'd you do it, Billy?

Pause.

Billy   Funny.

Ben Shephard   Anything else to add?

Billy   Yeah, it was fun. I wanted to put a smile on people's faces. Look, I'd had sixteen cans of lager, three grams of cocaine . . .

And I felt like a fucking . . .

King.

One

I know what you lot are thinking . . .

Why would you stick a flare up your arse? I get it. It's a strange manoeuvre. Not something that the common man would expect of you.

But when there are that many people, with all their eyes on you, you'll do anything to impress 'em. To win them over. And something changed that day, something snapped. Forever.

See, football starts with people.

I'm ten years old when my grandad leaves me with this beautiful vintage leather ball signed by *Sir Bobby Moore*.

Now, any football fan would kill to have such a thing but I'm just waiting to get down the park and smash the living daylights out of it with Adam.

Adam's my best mate. I fucking love him!

We met at school, both pretty quiet back then, last to get picked in PE kinda kids, but we bonded over our love of the game.

Saturday morning rolls around and we're practising our penalties in the park.

Me in goal. Adam winding one up. Concentration etched into his face, and BANG!

He swoops his foot beneath the ball, ballooning it . . .

right over my head,

right over the crossbar,

and right over this fence . . .

We watch as it rolls down a hill towards a lake, eventually dropping in and bobbing its way to the middle.

Adam doesn't know it's signed yet but when I tell him he almost kicks me in the cock.

The disbelief that I could use this *talisman* to just kick about the park.

He doesn't even lecture me on it, oh no, before I know it, he's off. Scaling the fence, down to his underpants, diving in headfirst. You'd think he was saving a drowning puppy.

By the time I get to the lake, he's already back at shore. Dripping head to toe. Covered in weeds and frogspawn.

He is furious with me. Using his jumper to dry off the ball.

The passion and the outrage on his little freckled face. I could tell that in that moment, what football meant to him.

He goes to hand it back to me, but I tell him to.

Billy   Keep it, mate. You deserve it. You'll look after it better than I can.

And he takes it, like you take money off your nan. You feel guilty . . . but you want it. He double checks with me.

Billy   Of course, it's all yours.

I tell him.

And then he says, 'It's ours'.

Beat.

And then he attacks me with the biggest hug, knocking me to the ground, soaking me in pond shit. Little prick!

That's what football was all about.

–

AFC WIMBLEDON!

Adam takes me to my first-ever game.

AFC Wimbledon versus Bristol Rovers.

I remember it clear as day.

We sit just to the left of the dugouts. Adam points to our manager, Terry Brown.

Billy   Oy, Terry! Give us a wave!

Terry Brown turns around and waves at us. We're part of the team, part of the action.

Two–all with five minutes left to play and, in a flash, our striker goes down in the box!

A referee's whistle sounds.

The referee gives a penalty!

We cling on to each other, holding our breath as he steps up, and . . .

Goal!

Right in the top corner! We're bouncing around like Tigger . . .

. . . on acid!

This was football.

The drama of it, the *theatricality* of it.

This was football.

The feeling of all our fans coming together, an entire community, calling the Bristolians . . .

Billy   Wankers!

He laughs as he remembers that time.

Adam and I, we share a lot of firsts. Our first beer. First house party. First World Cup. First time watching us lose a World Cup, summer BBQs, GCSEs . . .

When Mum dies, Adam and I go to our first funeral.

He held my hand . . .

Billy *catches himself being too sentimental.*

For a second!

He tells me it'll be okay. He tells me whatever happens, we'll always have football.

And that's all it was! Football. It's what defined my
happiness. It's what filled my soul with joy and occasionally
. . . despair.

–

A-level results day.

I'm stood next to Adam; he's shaking like a leaf, terrified of
not getting the grades he needs for his wanker banker
internship.

Mr Kripson comes and shakes his hand.

Mr Kripson   I think you'll be very pleased, young man.

And then he looks at me . . . hesitates . . . no handshake, no
nothing, just utters:

Mr Kripson   Have a *decent* life.

Bastard.

–

I'm eighteen and working in Dad's hair salon.

Him and mum set it up years ago. Just before she passed
away. It was their passion project.

The walls are littered with all their favourite artwork and
photographs. None of it really goes together or matches but
somehow, it works.

Dad's a creative, *artsy* kind of person. He wears corduroy and
has a little tash. Chats to the customers about anything and
everything. Tracey Emin? Phantom of the Opera? Politics?
You name it. My mum was exactly the same . . . without the
tash. Obviously.

He's also a workaholic, I mean he has to be, he's a small
business owner and that but he's needed an extra pair of
hands for years! Not for cutting hair but for the little jobs
like sweeping, making teas and coffees, and 'computer stuff'.
All the fun bits, you know?

But I try to do everything the way it should be done, to his standard.

The salon doorbell rings.

There's this one customer though, right . . . Mrs Richards. She comes in like clockwork. Every four Fridays.

She's a rat. Honest to God. She's got a face that folds over itself like a spunky tissue.

Billy   Would you like a cup of tea, Mrs Richards?

Mrs Richards   I thought you'd know my order by now.

I bite my tongue. She carries on . . .

Mrs Richards   Two sugars and a drop of milk.

I'm out the back, wondering whether to poison the bitch or not . . . but I make it to standard, bring it out, and watch as she swirls it around her wrinkly old cheeks.

Mrs Richards   Too weak. Do it again. What is the point of him working here if he can't even make tea?

Billy *shudders with anger.*

I want to say something.

You know. I feel like I should say *something*. But there are other customers watching, and to be honest . . .

I'm not brave enough.

Dad sees me tense up and tells me to take a break.

I go outside, cursing and fuming the hell of my nine to five.

Thank God it's Friday!

–

MATCHDAY

Every Saturday, I meet Adam at Monty's Café. 9 am. He is always on time.

Billy *gestures apologetically for his lateness!*

I'm not . . .

Best full English in the world. Eggs, bacon, hash browns. The works. It's a bean in a ramekin kind of place.

And there's this waitress there and I'm convinced she's giving me the eyes.

Adam reckons it's 'cause I keep staring at her, being creepy but she always makes a point of saying hi. Adam says: that's her job.

Monty's is where we chew the fat. Not the bacon but the fat from our weeks. You know, talk, like *really* talk.

My family, his dog. His family, my dog!

He tells me about his new job in the city, I tell him about . . . Mrs Richards. He laughs. Don't think he envies me.

He's content. At least, I thought he was.

The waitress comes over and gives us our breakfast for free, 'on the house', she says.

She definitely wants me to ask her out. Staring down at me, ready for some great chat and I say:

Billy   Thanking you very much, looking forward to our next visit.

Billy *explodes in embarrassment.*

Why the fuck did I say that?! It sounded right in my head, but it came out all weird!

One look at Adam and we're out of there. Legend.

He's good at that. Always getting us out of them awkward kinda situations. But he does ring every inch of piss out of me on our way to The Crown!

This is where we watch the early kick-off on the big screen.

Throw some darts, play some pool.

And most importantly, neck a few pints. Cheers.

He downs a pint.

Four lagers down and it's off to the game. Anything can happen. Sure, we're used to losing, but we're together.

Win, lose or draw . . . and it's back to The Crown.

And we're set for the lock-in.

There's this one group of lads right, we see 'em every week without fail. They're older than us. Thirties maybe.

One of them towers over the rest. He's bald and built like a brick shit . . . *mansion.*

He's got a voice that rings out across the entire pub. A *reverberating* motherfucker. Always has his mates in stitches.

We nickname him 'The King'.

I wonder what it's like to have that sort of power. That sort of respect.

After the game, them lot, they *own* the pool table. We don't dare put our quid on in case The King has something to say about it.

It's my round, I'm off to get our next beers. The pool table is located in this tight little spot, next to the bar . . . you gotta squeeze round it to order a drink.

But The King is playing, lining up his shot. So naturally, I stand back and wait.

Twenty seconds later and I'm still stood there like a fucking lemon. Waiting for him.

He pulls out, chalks his cue, and just as I see an opportunity to walk – he's lining up his shot again. Really taking his time. All of his mates look at each other. Knowingly.

I clock on, it's a power game. He's daring me to walk past.

So, as he lines up his shot for a third time. I take the risk. Tiptoeing around the back of his beefy mass. Suddenly, the cue pierces into my stomach, knocking me back into his pint.

Lager flies all over the shop.

I can feel the whole pub's eyes on me.

Adam's scratching his head.

Even Debs, the landlady, is saying a little prayer.

Wine Gum   It looks like you've ruined my shot.

Billy   Sorry, sorry. Sorry about that, Sir. What are you drinking, I'll get you another. I'll buy you two if you like!

I'm turning more middle class by the syllable.

Wine Gum   You're Wimbledon, ain't ya? Seen you at the home games.

Billy   Yes! Yeah, me and my mate Adam over here, season ticket holders for what is it . . . eight years now, so . . .!

His gaze starts to soften; his hardcore frown turns into a charismatic grin.

Wine Gum   Alright, I'll let you off. But how about you and your mate give me and Elton here a wager for them two pints you was talking about?

I look over at a slightly shorter bloke with glasses, who does in fact look like *Elton John*.

The King spots me trying to work him out.

Wine Gum   His name's not actually Elton, it's Dave! But he does look like the poofter.

Wine Gum *breaks out into a gigantic laugh that evolves into* **Billy**'s *awkward and timid laugh.*

He laughs at his own joke and like the Pied Piper, has us all laughing with him.

Adam and I share a cue between us. He's much better than me, pocketing our balls, one after the other.

Just the black ball left and Adam sticks it right in the corner pocket.

We high five . . . cautiously.

Wine Gum   Good game, lads! Elton, grab those Stellas. I'm Wine Gum by the way. Obviously, you know Elton. That's Rodney, Mrs Beaver and Chris Tingle. A pleasure to meet you, boys.

All of the lads welcome us, with the same: 'alright?'

Wine Gum   You boys up for a laugh then?

Billy   Yeah . . . Course.

Wine Gum   Here's a little something for ya then.

Wine Gum *pulls out a bag of cocaine from his pocket.*

–

Adam and I are stood, shoulder to shoulder, crammed into the pub loos, staring down at a small bag of white powder that Wine Gum has given us.

We're virgins. We have no idea what this is!

I reckon ketamine. Adam reckons meth.

Wait?

Meth?!

Billy   Fucking *Breaking Bad,* it's obviously not meth, Adam!

We Google it!

We Talk to Frank.

And we come to the conclusion; well, we're 99 per cent sure that this is cocaine.

Billy   I'll do it if you do it?

You first he says.

So I lick my finger, dab it in the bag and sniff the white.

Adam looks at me, looks down at the bag, and back at me and says he might do some later.

I tell him he's gotta do some now! Otherwise, he's a shit mate. I'm nervous, I need him to do it with me. He agrees, reluctantly.

–

After some time, I feel, well, I feel nothing. For a moment, I start thinking maybe it was one of those dud batches that Frank told us about.

And then . . .

BANG!

A massive rush of energy washes over **Billy**.

My God . . . I feel like *Elon Musk*!

The rush, the buzz, the energy. I'm chatting off ears left, right, and centre.

Debs brings out the karaoke machine! Elton sings 'Tiny Dancer'.

Nothing seems off the cards. I even ask Wine Gum if I can have some more!

Wine Gum   More?! More?!

He jokes before sorting me out.

Adam and I have a turn on the karaoke machine, we sing our favourite tune.

He sings 'Tubthumping' by Chumbawamba, but gets a few of the lyrics wrong.

I get knocked down, banana bap again!

Na na na na na

–

We are in a club! Wine Gum has dragged us to Infernos.

Wine Gum   The best club in the country. Pure cheese.

The Charlie's pumping right through me, making me pull out dance moves I've only ever dreamed of.

The moonwalk.

The sprinkler.

The robot.

You name it, I'm on it.

And I shit you not, that waitress from Monty's is in here. She's all made up, a million quid. She's looking over at me. I've forgotten all about that chat this morning, all about that slightly awkward version of me.

I'm gearing up to make my move.

When I'm distracted by a random lad in a rugby shirt who comes up to me. His name's Finnian.

Finnian   Oi, chaps, Brownley over here reckons you couldn't chop a pint.

I have no idea what that means but before you know it, I embarrass myself, dribbling lager all over my top but I don't care.

Adam's drunk. Really drunk. I put my arm around him and go to kiss him on the cheek but in that moment, he has a rebirth of life, turns, and we kiss on the lips.

Fucking hilarious!

I find Wine Gum and the others having a fag in the smoking area.

From the other side, I see her, the girl from the café and she's talking to . . . Finnian.

I can feel myself getting a bit green. 'That should be me', I think.

Wine Gum   The thing is Billy; you don't get anything in this life by standing there like a fucking lemon.

Wine Gum's right. I've got to make my move.

'Reach for the Stars' by S Club 7 begins to play from inside the club.

I can hear S Club 7 playing from the inside.

I follow that rainbow shining over her and strut across, Finnian turns to me . . . she's smiling, all elegantly.

Finnian   Can't you see I'm a bit busy, mate?

Billy   I want to speak to her.

Finnian   Finders keepers.

Billy   Finders keepers? You don't own her; she's not a Mars Bar!

And he shoves me, getting all lairy. For a moment I feel like I did when Mrs Richards was pushing me around.

I see Wine Gum and the other lads looking at over, ready to jump in.

It steadies me up.

Billy   I wouldn't, mate.

I say, signalling towards them.

And he backs off. Scurries away. See ya later, rugby boy.

And I'm dancing with her. With Daisy! That's her name.

I feel unstoppable. Like the whole world is at my feet. And just as I lean in to kiss her . . .

I get a tap on the shoulder.

Bouncer.

Adam's been kicked out for chucking his guts up.
Cockblocker.

We're sat on the pavement outside the kebabby covered in
donner juices. Adam starts crying, bloody mess. I don't think
he could handle it. The booze. The drugs.

But for the first time in my life, I felt like I was in control.

–

Two

Billy *chants to the tune of 'You Are My Sunshine', inserting
Daisy's name for sunshine.*

The days at the salon start to feel shorter.

The weekends come and go quickly.

We've been going to the games with Wine Gum. He keeps
talking about official induction and how it's something we've
got to earn. But never says how.

Daisy meets me after work.

Dad keeps offering her free haircuts. Every time she's there,
he's all . . .

Dad   Isn't my Billy lucky to have a girl like you in his life?

It makes *my* toes curl! But *she* deals with it well.

I take her for dinner! Well, it's nothing fancy, we just go
down the chippy.

But she doesn't mind. She's a pretty simple person actually.

He catches himself.

Not in a rude way!

She just likes me for me. It's nice.

We sit and eat it in Wimbledon Park. She tells me all about her life.

Daisy is a singer-songwriter. Moved here from Bristol, she only works at Monty's as a filler whilst looking for places to gig.

I joke about my first-ever football game and how we called the Bristol fans wankers. She laughs.

I point out the lake that Adam saved that ball from. I tell her about the salon and how it's not really what I wanna be doing but it's alright for now.

I get a call from Adam. He's wired on a Wednesday, down the pub with Wine Gum. He begs me to go.

And here's the nuts thing: Daisy encourages me! Like she fully just says 'Go be with your friends down the pub' . . .

The dream!

No, no . . . but I call her when I get home. We talk for hours, barely sleeping before work but I've never had that before, and it feels . . . it feels . . .

Billy *tries to find the words to describe it but*

He can't.

–

Billy *breaks out into a chant to the tune of 'Bless 'Em All' by George Formby Jr, changing the words to 'Fuck 'em all'.*

FUCK EM ALL! FUCK EM ALL!

CHELSEA WEST HAM AND MILLWALL

CAUSE WE ARE THE WOMBLES AND WE ARE THE BEST.

WE ARE THE WOMBLES SO FUCK ALL THE REST.

FUCK EM ALL, FUCK EM ALL.

MATCHDAY

Grimsby.

Away.

Someone else's territory. Someone else's turf.

They're winning two–one, their fans are leaning over at us and pointing specifically at Wine Gum who's giving it the biggun.

Grimsby Fans   YOU FAT BASTARD, YOU FAT BASTARD

They chant at him. Inflating him with hot rage.

Wine Gum   Come on then, I'll take the lot of you on. I'll eat ya fucking babies!

Right. It's a really questionable response . . . but he has no filter for what's coming out his mouth.

We lose the game two–one. All the lads are focused on Wine Gum's next move as we walk out the ground.

Wine Gum   If we can't do the business on the pitch, we gotta do it off.

Adam and I have no idea what that means but we're being lead well away from Grimsby train station, down some back roads.

It's quiet for a moment.

Something is brewing. About to begin.

Wine Gum   Any moment now, their boys will come round this corner. Billy, Adam, get fucking stuck in.

I look across at Adam. He looks petrified. I am too. We've never been in a fight before. He mouths across, suggesting we go back to the train station.

But before I have time to respond, six Grimsby fans are coming at us, effing and jeffing.

Billy (*nervously*)   COME ON THEN!

We watch as they catapult themselves into each other. Wine Gum is in there, using his arms as propellers, knocking back their lads.

I don't want him to see us bottle it.

Adam grabs my arm; I can feel him shaking.

With all the lager and cocaine in our system, this is intense.

One of their boys, breaks from the group and decks Adam.

I watch as this fella is stood over him, kicking him repeatedly.

Something clicks in me, the fear evaporates and replaced with pure, unadulterated fury.

Without hesitation, I'm on him. Tackling him off Adam.

He smacks up at me catching me on the eye but then I flip him round.

And one, two, three, smashing him in the face.

It feels . . . it feels . . .

. . . fucking great.

–

On the train journey home, Wine Gum officially inducts us into the firm. That's what he calls our group!

Wine Gum   You both got stuck in and fought like warriors, well done.

And it's official. We're in the WhatsApp group chat.

–

Can't say Dad's best pleased when I turn up to work with a black eye.

I don't tell him why, course, I just tell him that I slipped and fell over when celebrating our goal and landed on a barrier.

Dad   You can't let Daisy see you like this, you look like you've been in the Battle of the Somme.

Billy   . . . the what?

He's right, though.

So I call Daisy and tell her I'm not feeling great. I ask if we can take a raincheck on dinner.

She agrees but says I gotta make it up to her.

So Dad gives me a bit of money to take her to the theatre. I have no idea what to book so I let him sort it for me. He's into all that West End bollocks.

He books us two tickets to the Saturday martini performance of Lez Miserables.

Plan is, meet the boys, watch the game then head to meet Daisy.

That's when Dad tells me that:

Dad   Martini is pronounced matinee

and

Dad   matinee means afternoon performance.

Billy   Why would you book something when you know I'm at football?

He claims he didn't know, says it might be nice to do something else for a change.

Bullshit. He knew.

And in hindsight, I think he was doing it on purpose.

—

MATCHDAY

Apart from, I'm not there, I'm swapping chanting for sitting in silence.

Les Misérables, as Daisy tells me it's pronounced, is about some French revolution that apparently happened.

Billy   Sorry, scuse me, sorry, yeah we're just in the middle over there, yeah, thanks.

The good news is, you're allowed to drink beer inside this stadium.

I keep my phone on, notifications for the game at the ready.

The lights go down and the curtain rises.

So there's this fella, right. His names Jean Valjean and he's stolen a loaf of bread.

2460 . . . ONE NIL TO THE DONS! I CAN'T SUPPRESS MY EXCITEMENT.

Daisy snatches it off me, apparently it's 'disrespectful to the performers'.

Anyway, so there's this other bloke Javert – he's a policeman and he's chasing Valjean the bread man around. There's another guy Thernadier. He's Wine Gum, isn't he. Master of the house and all that. He's got this kid that is well unlooked after for so Jean Valjean comes in and rescues her and they're all singing and dancing and shit. It's literally like being down The Crown.

They're all screaming about there being one day more and to be honest with you . . .

The drama of it, the theatricality of it, I'm getting into this!

Billy *stands up and applaudes.*

At half-time.

Billy *asks a member of the audience what half-time is called in 'theatre'.*

The interval, I mean . . .

Daisy disappears and comes back with . . . two ice creams!
Nice one! But nothing to eat it with . . .

A spoon in the lid?

He checks the lid of the ice cream.

FUCK OFF, IT'S LIKE NARNIA IN HERE!

Daisy gives me my phone back. I check the group chat to see
Adam doing a line of cocaine off of Elton John's . . .

Oh no, that is his forehead. Phew. It all looks a bit forced, I
bet Adam is missing me.

Wine Gum captions it 'What a real fan looks like'.

I hide the message from Daisy.

The second act begins and I'm trying to keep up with it all. I
keep thinking about all the fun I'm missing out on but
suddenly they're all fighting up on stage.

It's back and forth, back and forth and then Javert sneaks
into Jean Valjean's camp. And there's this kid who is like
'YOU ARE DEFO A POLICEMAN!' and rats him out.

Billy   WELL GO ON, JEAN VALJEAN, YOU FUCKING
NUTCASE, SMACK HIM IN THE MOUTH.

But he doesn't! Jean Valjean lets Javert go. After all that shit,
he just forgives him. And it's really hot in this theatre.

I wonder what the score is. Are Adam and Wine Gum
getting on – not that they don't, but I'm usually the
connective tissue, you know? I hope Wine Gum still includes
me next week.

I look back at the stage and Javert is standing on this bridge
and he's singing this song. Kind of talking his way through
it. It's all quite a . . . a bit.

And it's proper stuffy in here and

I'm starting to sweat and

I let go of Daisy's hands

'cause mine are so clammy and

I hope she doesn't take it the wrong way and

my heart is beating really fast and

the band is getting louder and

my ears are ringing and

I feel a bit dizzy and

Javert JUMPS

Ends it all

And it's just –

Billy *scrambles for the exit.*

Billy   Fuck. Sorry, 'scuse me, sorry, yeah, thanks, need some air, thank you, sorry.

I'm stood outside the theatre, leaning up against a wall. Daisy follows me out, she looks confused, worried . . .

Billy   I'm fine, Daisy

Billy   I said, I'm fine.

Billy *turns to the audience. Doing his best to cover his embarrassment and reassure them.*

I'm fine.

–

Billy *chants to the tune of 'Can't Help Falling in Love' by Elvis Presley.*

Billy *does a line of cocaine.*

–

MATCHDAY

Right, back to real life. I meet Adam in Monty's Café, 9 am.

He is . . . late, he's never late.

When he gets there, he asks about the theatre. How it was. Genuinely interested.

I lie. I don't want him knowing what happened . . . telling the others.

Daisy's been acting strange, too. She's a lot more cautious around me.

Keeps 'checking in', ever since . . .

'Theatre-gate'.

Les Mis is the last time I miss the football.

We finish up at Monty's and it's down The Crown.

Pint? Yes, please.

Pint, pint, pint, gear, pint

Football

A win?!

–

Billy *chants to the tune of 'Achy Breaky Heart' by Billy Ray Cyrus.*

DON'T TAKE ME HOME
PLEASE DON'T TAKE ME HOME
I JUST DON'T WANNA GO TO WORK
I WANNA STAY HERE
DRINKING ALL THE BEER
PLEASE DON'T, PLEASE DON'T
TAKE ME HOME

Chanting is like its own drug, right? It's like blowing all the cobwebs out from your insides and prepares you. To be heard. Combine that with all the lager and the cocaine . . . it makes you forget about . . .

real life.

–

Suddenly, momentum begins to build, and **Billy** *has a new lease of life, a new buzz, a burst of energy.*

MATCHDAY

Hartlepool away.

Proud North-Eastern bunch. Polite enough crowd.

Until they beat us three–nil.

Sending us 250 miles home with nothing.

Wine Gum doesn't settle for it.

Wine Gum   We gotta let them know who we are. Don't show weakness.

Right hook. Upper cut, crack them in the nuts. Adrenaline rush.

Knuckles bleed on the train journey home. Don't feel it. Another line.

Adam can't finish his crate of beers. Amateur!

Take Daisy for dinner the next day. Feeling ropey. She barely eats anything. I clean her plate for her. Can't waste good food.

Beat.

The next week, meet Adam at Monty's Café. 9 am. He wants to talk about something but there's no time.

It's MATCHDAY!

Home to Cambridge.

The posh boys. At least, I'm pretty sure they're posh.

'Cause of all that university bollocks.

They don't fight like their posh.

Another black eye.

Beat.

MATCHDAY

The lads are in Liverpool. Tranmere Rovers.

Wine Gum   It would be rude not to!

Win the game.

Win the fight.

Feeling alive. Feeling part of something.

Party time on the train journey home. Adam's being boring. Glued to his phone.

I finish my crate of beers. 'Cause I'm a fucking pro.

–

Billy *spirals, repeating the same mantra repeatedly.*

MATCHDAY! PINT, PINT, CHANTING, PINT, GEAR, PINT! FIGHT!

He loses himself in the repetition until finally . . .

MATCHDAY

We're away to Milton Keynes.

Milton Keynes are our biggest rivals.

Adam doesn't come. Apparently busy with 'work commitments'.

Of all the games to miss.

Wine Gum   You're better than him anyway. More of a laugh.

So, I'm doing a line of coke off the toilet seat on the train up.

The game ends nil–nil. I can't even remember it. Not 'cause it was boring but we spent most of our time in the concourse.

The police make our fans walk the long way round to the station.

BUT WE AIN'T HAVING THAT!

We sneak in with their fans.

Everyone's pushing, one of 'em pushes Wine Gum a bit too hard and it sets off the bomb.

Next thing you know, everyone's pushing each other. Shouting in each other's faces.

Pint, pint, chanting, pint, gear, pint! Fight!

Billy *is struck by an MK fan.*

One of 'em smashes me in the ribs, I can feel it crack. I'm on the ground looking up at hundreds of people walking past until the heel of a Doc Marten . . .

sends me to sleep.

–

I wake up in A and E with a couple of broken ribs and a very sore head.

Wine Gum messages me saying they had to leave early to make it look like an accident.

The hospital is keen to get me discharged quickly so Dad picks me up. No way he's gonna believe this was another,

Dad   Celebrating a goal incident?

On the car journey home. We sit in silence. Just like we used to when Mum was dying.

It's not until we're all the way onto the M25, when he says

Dad   Hey Bill, maybe you should focus on work for a little while, ay?

And that's enough, enough to say how it really is:

Billy   What work, Dad? The work *you* want me to do? The work you *need* me to do, because you still haven't learned how to use a fucking computer? Mum would be embarrassed.

–

Turns out, not even Dad can focus on work. We're placed into a 'National Lockdown'.

Dad's got asthma so he's shielding, no one comes in, no one goes out.

Can't see Daisy so we just FaceTime. Not really saying much, just staring at each other down the screen.

Wine Gum doesn't think the rules are for him. Him and the boys keep partying around each other's houses.

Adam and I play Xbox, he seemed happier somehow. I think he missed the old days, when it was just me and him.

I sit alone in my room, waiting for the weekend.

Waiting for football.

Waiting for my life back.

I'd even take a shift at the salon. I watch old games on YouTube. I call Wine Gum. He sorts me out with a bit of packet and drops it off to me. The gear helps the days move quicker.

Billy *does a line as 'Jerusalem' plays.*

He finds his bucket hat and his England flag which he wraps around himself as the COVID lockdown passes.

–

June 2021

We are back!

The first games to be played in front of crowds are England's Euro 2020 games. Played in 2021.

But most importantly, almost all of them are being played here – in Ol' Blighty.

Wine Gum is buzzing.

Wine Gum   First tournament here since ninety-six, before you were born, Billy! See you at The Crown.

It's coming home!

Southgate cruises us through the group stages. We watch every game in The Crown and celebrate into the early hours, except Adam who keeps cancelling last minute.

But that don't matter!

'Cause the sun is out, everyone is coming out from hibernation and back into existence.

And Daisy comes to the salon to tell us that she's booked her first headline gig! She's buzzing so I'm buzzing, so Dad is buzzing and even Mrs Richards is cracking a smile . . . it's really great. Honestly, I'm so happy for her . . .

It's just, England get drawn to Germany . . .

Wine Gum   You can't miss it, Bill. It's fucking Germany, the Holy Grail!

Right, international football is different. No more fighting. Let bygones be bygones and celebrate this great nation.

Wine Gum   As long as there's no Gerries around.

Wine Gum books us a spot at a pub near Wembley. Wants to soak up the atmosphere.

Daisy isn't on until 10 pm which gives me more than enough time to get there after the game. Unless it goes to penalites, of course . . .

Adam says he's busy. Fucking busy, it's Germany!

29 June 2021

England 2 Germany 0

Crowd cheers. England have beaten Germany.

Commentator   It's finally happened. England beat Germany at a major tournament!

FUCK OFF. FUCK. OFF.

He's only gone and done it. Southgate has actually beaten Germany.

We race our way to celebrate with the hundreds of people on Wembley Way. The atmosphere is insane!

I grab a few cans of lager from the Co-op!

Wine Gum thinks it's a good laugh to grab a bottle of Prosecco, climb up onto this bus shelter and spray it over everyone.

I grab my phone to get a photo of him and . . .

Twelve missed calls from Daisy?

Shit.

—

I take the tube across the city. Straight up to the bar where Daisy's playing.

Billy   Mate, please let me in, yes I know you're shut but I just need to see my girlfriend. She was performing tonight. And I need to help her. Help her pack up.

The bouncer finally lets me in.

The lights are off. Barmaid flipping the stools up onto the tables and Daisy's there, packing up her guitar.

She sees me come in. Ignores me. Just zips up her case.

I get closer. Suddenly her eyes flick towards me.

Billy   Dais! The tubes were fucked. And . . . and well, I might have accidentally stayed for a drink or two but I'm here now and someone must have filmed it . . . Dais?

She looks at me. She smiles. Tells me it's okay. I know it's not okay.

She says she's relieved. Glad to be rid of me.

Then she tells me that Adam was at her gig which really fucks me off to be honest because he said he was busy and –

But before I have time to kick off, she's at the door,

'Adam misses you', she says.

And then she's gone and I'm alone . . . lathered in sticky Prosecco.

–

Wednesday 7 July 2021

England 2 Denmark 1

Commentator   THEY'VE DONE IT, THEY'VE ONLY GONE AND DONE IT. THIS IS ENGLAND'S NIGHT. THE LONG, LONG WAIT IS OVER. THE EMOTIONAL, SOMETIMES EXHAUSTING JOURNEY CONTINUES. ENGLAND TWO DENMARK ONE AND THEY'RE HEADING TO THEIR FIRST FINAL SINCE SIXTY-SIX.

–

Sunday 11 July 2021

The European Championship Final

On the morning of the final, Adam suggests that we go to Monty's Café, for old times' sake.

Now he wants to pipe up. Says he got stuff to talk to me about.

But I'm not going anywhere near that café, not with Daisy working there. Anyway, Wine Gum has the perfect itinerary sorted.

Wine Gum   The game starts at 8 pm so we will meet at 7 . . . am. First tube out of Wimbledon. The mightiest of pub crawls. Then to Wembley Way, where we will storm the stadium and see England beat them Italian wankers.

Adam joins us for once. Glory hunter. He's quiet all morning. Probably guilty about his secret little rendezvous he's been having. Doesn't speak to me about it once.

It's so early in the morning and I've never seen London like it. We're singing chants on the tube.

Billy *chants to the tune of 'She'll Be Coming Round the Mountain When She Comes'.*

YOU CAN STICK YOUR FUCKING PASTA UP YOUR ARSE!

Adam doesn't join in.

Who cares?

We're stood at the top of Wembley Park tube station, overlooking the glory of Wembley Way.

There's a thick fog of smoke like a halo over the thousands of bodies.

We run off to join them like kids being let into a jungle gym.

And everyone's acting like animals, it feels incredible, you can do whatever you want because everyone else is doing exactly that.

We're the die-hards.

Proud to be here.

Proud to be one.

Proud to be English.

Three lions on our shirt.

Hoping and praying that this will be the night that ends all the hurt.

My turn to do something crazy, my turn to be seen.

To walk upon England's mountains gr –

Billy *is suddenly halted in what he's doing.*

Adam stops me. He tells me that what I'm about to do isn't a very good idea.

Billy   What do you know about good ideas? You've been quiet all morning, don't tell me what to do, mate.

To walk upon England's mountains gr –

He is halted for a second time.

He stops me again, telling me it's a *stupid* idea. Then he asks me why, why would I wanna do such a thing . . .

Billy   THIS FLARE IS GOING UP MY BUM AND WHY? WHY! BECAUSE IT'S FUCKING FUN!

'This is why Daisy broke up with you', he says. Tells me I take things too far. That I don't have any time for anyone but myself.

Billy   Oh, you'd know why, wouldn't you? Sneaking off to her gig, spending time with her behind my back. Come on, Adam, if you wanted my sloppy seconds, you just had to say!

He says that I've got it wrong, that I don't know him anymore, it's been that long since I spoke to him about anything other than football or lager or beers or –

Billy   I've got it wrong?! She told me. Look, if you're gonna be so gay about everything, why don't you just go home.

Beat.

And so, he leaves, pushing his way through the crowd, looking for an exit.

Broken.

Good riddance . . .

I pull my pants down as the crowd starts to cheer.

Wine Gum cracks open his twenty-fourth beer!

FOR ENGLAND.

FOR ST GEORGE.

AND FOR HARRY MAGUIRE!

–

Three

Inside Wembley Stadium.

Rodney, Mrs Beaver, Elton John, Chris Tingle, Wine Gum and me storm the turnstiles at Wembley. The steward just waves us through. She don't get paid enough to stop us.

Bukayo Saka is stood over the penalty that defines our history.

Southgate reckons this is a clever idea.

We cling onto each other. Holding our breath as he steps . . .

I think of Adam.

And then . . .

Saka misses.

it's over . . .

We let go of each other . . . we collapse . . . England collapses.

Wine Gum   Every fucking time.

On the way out of the ground, we are sombre. Drunk, high, but sombre.

Wine Gum is fuming.

Wine Gum   Why would he let Saka take it? He's not even English, is he?

–

As we walk back towards the tube station. I spot a little boy. He's with his dad and he's wearing an Italy shirt.

I think about the joy he must be feeling; it reminds me of when me and Adam were younger.

But he don't look happy, he looks scared.

Wine Gum barges past them looking for a reaction. The dad doesn't rise to it. Wine Gum gets all in his face.

The little boy bursts into tears, tugging at his dad's arm.

I push Wine Gum back!

Wine Gum   Who are you pushing, you little cunt? What is the point of you being here, if you won't stand with us against these –

Wine Gum carries on. I stop listening. A million and one things are racing through my mind.

He was just a kid.

Who loved football.

This was supposed to be the happiest moment of his life.

And yet, there's this man, this 'king'. So big, so tall but in that moment, he looked so small.

Like a tiny little sweetie.

A *wine gum*.

I laugh . . .

Billy *gets punched in the face.*

I take the hit. I'm down on the ground looking up at this oversized toddler screaming down at me as Rodney and Elton John wrestle him away.

I can hear Elton say:

Elton John   Leave it, Steve. He's a wanker.

–

The morning after.

Chris Kamara   So, why'd you do it, Billy?

Pause.

Billy   Funny.

Ben Shephard   Anything else to add?

Billy   Yeah, it was fun. I wanted to put a smile on people's faces. Look, I'd had sixteen cans of lager, three grams of cocaine . . .

And I felt like a fucking . . .

King.

Ben Shephard   Whoa! Okay, thank you very much for your call! Sorry about the strong language there. That was Mr Billy Kinley, the bum flare man. We want to hear your thoughts . . . is Billy just another example of English football fans spoiling our reputation? It's been a great tournament! Why can't we just focus on the game?

Chris Kamara   I know, Ben, it is such a shame, I mean what was he thinking?

Ben Shephard   We're here to take your calls on 063 482 114 . . .

Radio show fades out as **Billy** *begins to reflect.*

Photos spread across the internet. Everyone knows the bum flare man. But Billy Kinley feels alone.

He sits for a while, thinking about what to do next. He picks up his phone, and dials.

It rings.

It rings again.

Adam Voicemail   Hi! This is Adam, I'm either busy or I don't want to talk to you. Either way, leave a message!

Billy *pauses, wondering what to say or whether he can say anything at all.*

He doesn't.

He hangs up.

And it's not long after that I find out, how alone someone else was feeling.

Beat.

Epilogue

Billy *puts on a black suit jacket, speaking from a piece of paper.*

Billy   Hi, I'm Billy. Helen asked me if I'd say a few words. This is . . . It's a shock. Adam was my best mate. We had great times together. He loved his football and his family and his dog. We used to play down the park all the time. He took me to my first Wimbledon game. We used to spend time down at a café together where we'd chat. We always clung on to each other . . . To be honest . . . I didn't really know that this was happening to him . . . It was . . .

He folds up his speech.

I didn't know 'cause I didn't . . . well, I didn't bother asking. Because as long as we were having 'fun', I assumed everything was alright. But everything wasn't alright. And maybe . . . I dunno, maybe we weren't having fun at all. For you, football was just something to do on a Saturday, a passion, a time for us to make memories and I took that away from you because I wasn't happy like you were, I needed something more, I couldn't deal with that pathetic version of me. I wanted to feel bigger, better than other people. So instead of being truthful about my life, I ran away and tried dragging you with me. The last thing you asked me was why, why would you stick a flare up your arse? And I didn't know how to answer it then, but I think I do now . . . to belong, to be powerful – like a king? Like Wine Gum? But now I know what he is . . . a thug, a weakling. And now that I think about it, mate, we were kings once – in them long days in the park, and Monty's where we had them amazing conversations. Before I got caught up in . . . nothingness. We should have done it more. I feel guilty for not doing it more. I should have been there for you. I should have let you be there for me. And I'm sorry for that, Adam. I really am.

–

After the funeral, Helen – Adam's mum – hands me a box of things she thought he'd want me to have.

Daisy is at the funeral. She holds my hand, for a second.

She tells me he had a lot of things he'd want me to hear. She invites me to Monty's to talk it all through.

Dad is constantly trying to make me laugh, make me smile. He even shuts the salon for a few days which he's never done, not out of choice anyway.

He offers to take me to a Wimbledon game.

I ask if we can go to the theatre instead. He prefers that idea.

A few months pass and I still haven't met Daisy for the chat. I can't, I can't hear her say it's all my fault. I know it is.

One night, I open the box Helen gave me.

Billy *pulls out the signed Bobby Moore ball.*

It's in better condition than I ever remembered it being in.

He took such good care of it, like I knew he would.

And I realise that this isn't all about me, nor should it be. It's about him. So, I call Daisy and we meet at Monty's Café.

She tries to explain how Adam was feeling, she tries to make the whole thing easier. It's not enough, nothing will ever be enough.

But it's something.

The manager agrees to let me put up a shelf, next to mine and Adam's table.

I write on our ball.

To the conversations, we should have had.

'Stars' from Les Mis plays as the lights fade out.

Blackout.

The End.

ALTERNATE RADIO HOST SCRIPT

One

Radio Host   Welcome back to Fanatic about Footie with me, Simon Jules! Well, despair sweeps the nation this morning as last night's Euros final against Italy ended in bitter disappointment. We're joined now by Mr Billy Kinley, pictured on Wembley Way yesterday doing something pretty explosive. (*Forceful laugh.*) Care to explain to the listener what that was?

Billy   Yeah, I stuck a flare up my bum.

Radio Host   You certainly did, young man, and it is quite the story! You've got over 50,000 likes on Instagram! And hashtag bum flare man is still trending on Twitter!

Billy   That's right, Si. I guess I'm a bit of a cult hero.

Radio Host   Can I just ask you, Billy, what does it feel like when you're sticking a flare up your arse?

Billy   I can't really explain it . . .

Beat.

Radio Host   It looks like he hasn't got the words . . .

Billy *quotes a key line from the movie 'Billy Elliot' about losing who you are.*

Radio Host   Is that Billy Elliot?

Billy   No, my name's Kinley. It's Billy Kin-Leyyyyy.

Radio Host   So, why'd you do it, Billy?

Billy *takes a second to reply as he questions this himself.*

Billy   Funny.

Radio Host   Anything else to add?

Billy   Yeah, it was fun. I wanted to put a smile on people's faces. Look, I'd had sixteen cans of lager, three grams of cocaine . . .

And I felt like a fucking . . .

King.

Three

Radio Host   So, why'd you do it, Billy?

Billy *takes a second to reply as he questions this himself.*

Billy   Funny.

Radio Host   Anything else to add?

Billy   Yeah, it was fun. I wanted to put a smile on people's faces. Look, I'd had sixteen cans of lager, three grams of cocaine . . .

And I felt like a fucking . . .

King.

Radio Host   Whoa! Thank you very much for your call! That was Mr Billy Kinley, the bum flare man. We want to hear your thoughts . . . is Billy just another example of English football fans spoiling our reputation? It's been a great tournament! Why can't we just focus on the game? Surely it's these kinds of antics that help perpetuate the abhorrent racism we see in today's game . . .

Radio fades out.

For a complete listing of
Methuen Drama titles, visit:
www.bloomsbury.com/drama

Follow us on X and keep up to date with
our news and publications
@MethuenDrama